EXPLORE THE WORLD

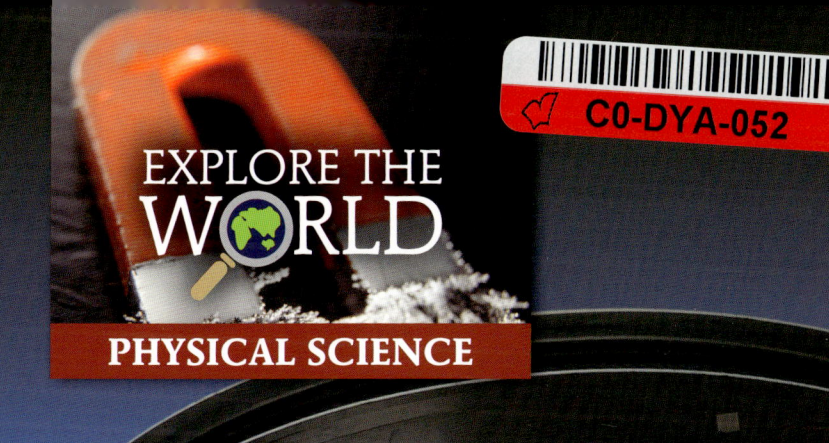

PHYSICAL SCIENCE

Pulleys
Simple Machines in Our World

MATTHEW HUGO

TABLE OF CONTENTS

What Is a Pulley?	2
How Do Pulleys Work?	4
Where Can We Find Pulleys?	6
Pulleys: Past and Present	16
Glossary/Index	20

PIONEER VALLEY EDUCATIONAL PRESS, INC

WHAT IS A PULLEY?

A pulley is a rope wrapped around a wheel. It is a simple machine that can be used to move something heavy. The rope fits into the **groove** of the wheel and one end of the rope is **attached** to a heavy object.

PARTS OF A PULLEY

rope

groove

wheel

HOW DO PULLEYS WORK?

Did you know that if you pull down on one end of a pulley you can lift a heavy **load** on the other end?

We use pulleys because they help us move heavy objects up, down, and sideways. They are also good for helping us move objects that are in places that are hard to reach.

5

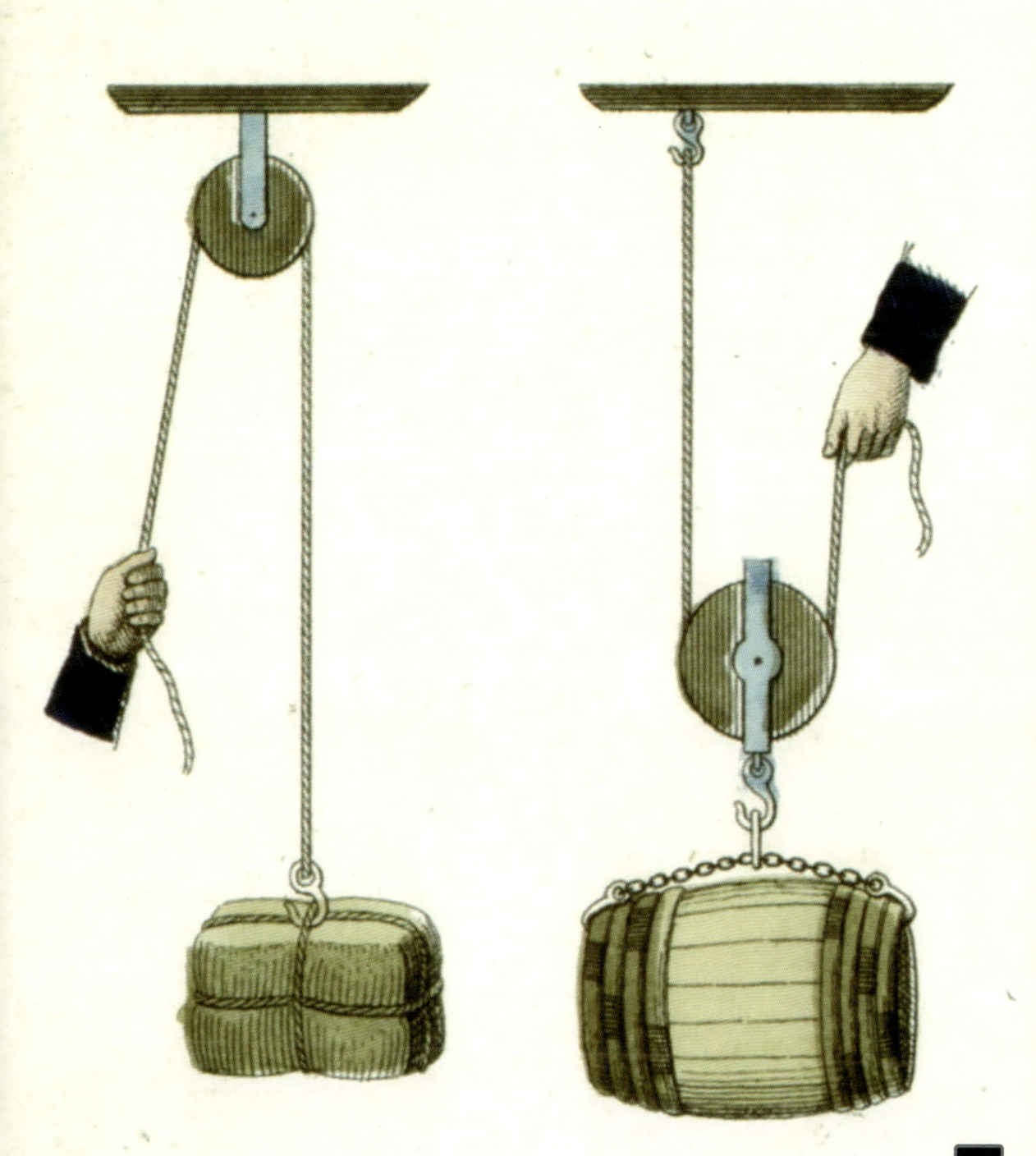

WHERE CAN WE FIND PULLEYS?

People use pulleys to get water out of wells. A rope connected to a bucket goes over a pulley and down a well that has water at the bottom. A person pulls on the rope to lift the heavy bucket of water.

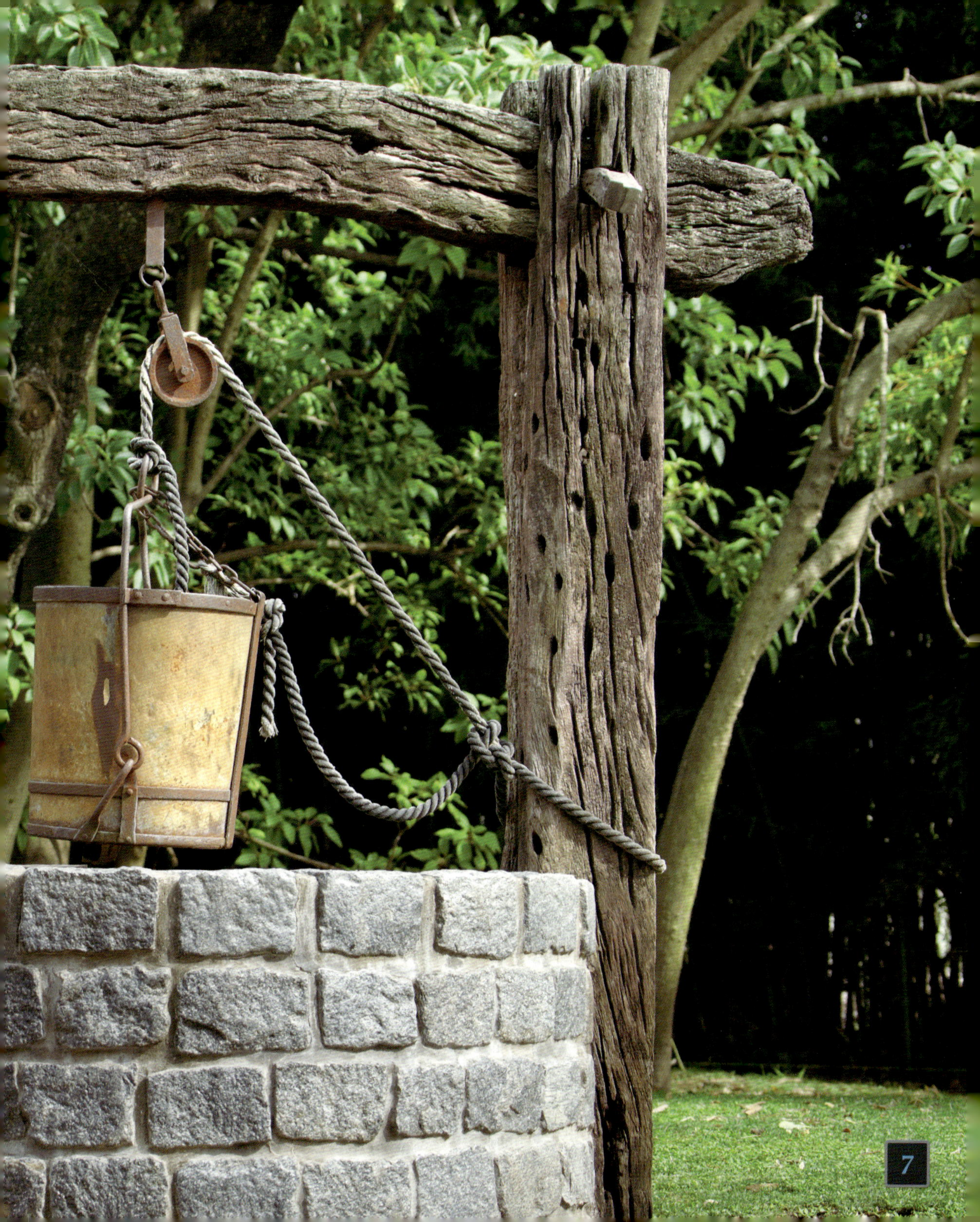

Window **blinds** can be lifted or lowered by using a small pulley. The cord goes over a very small wheel. As you pull down on the cord, the blind goes up. As you **release** the cord, the blind goes down.

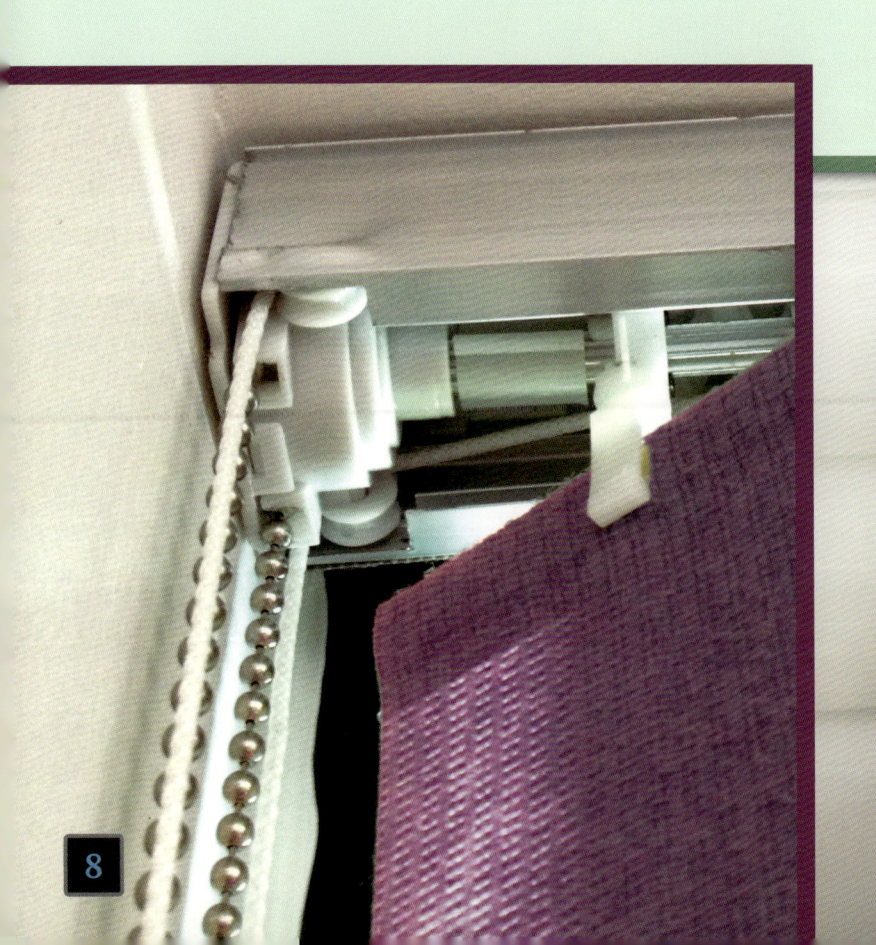

9

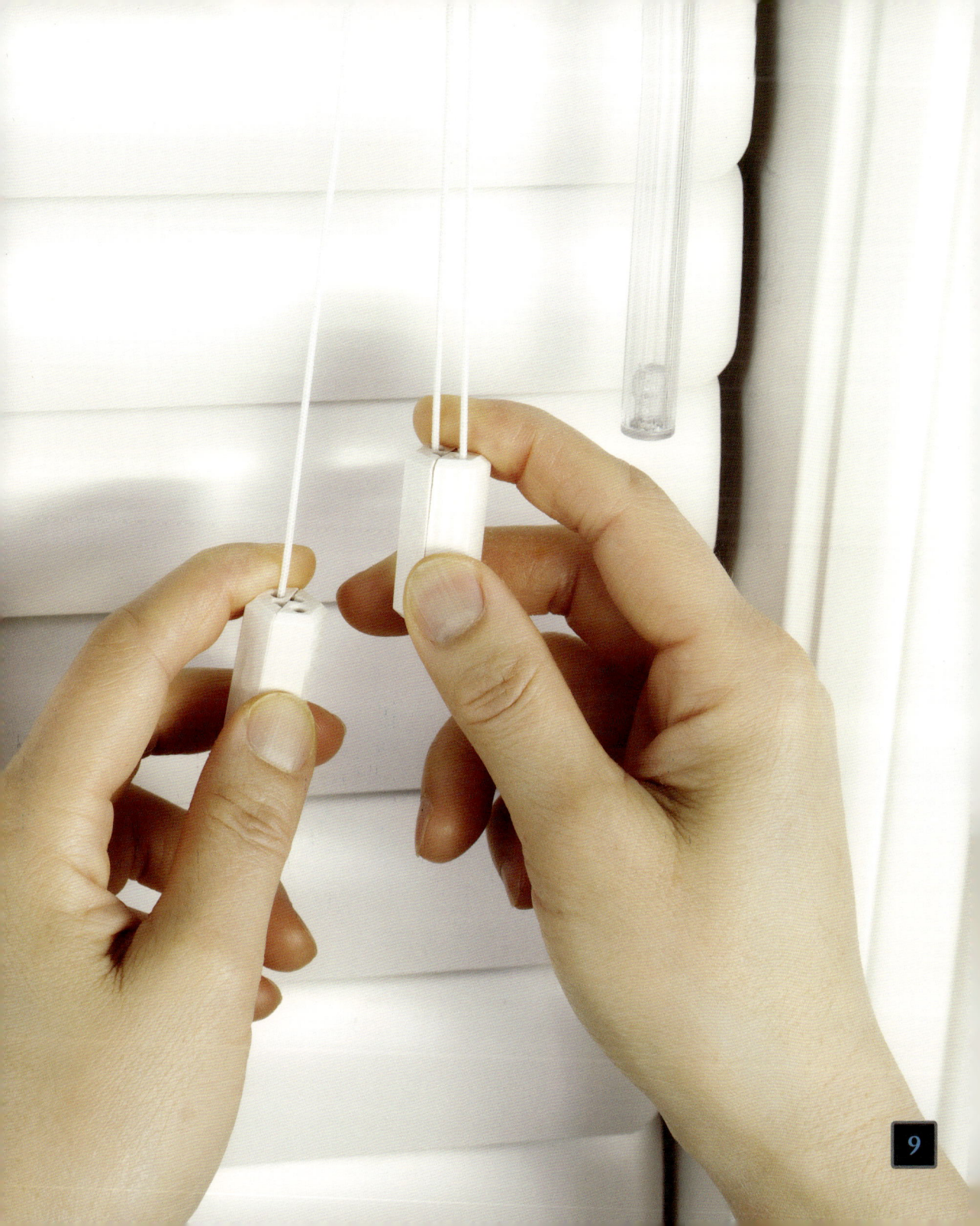

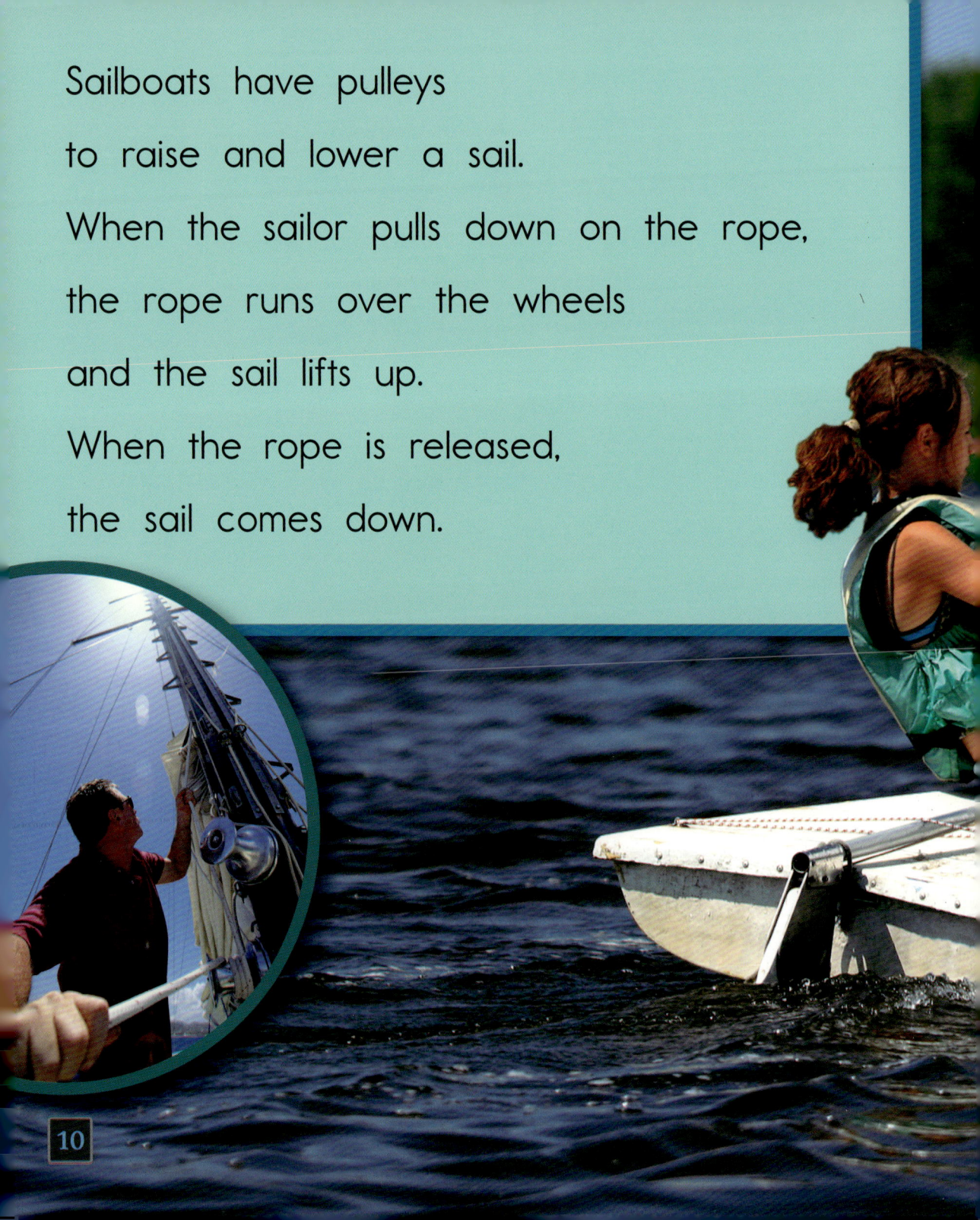

Sailboats have pulleys
to raise and lower a sail.
When the sailor pulls down on the rope,
the rope runs over the wheels
and the sail lifts up.
When the rope is released,
the sail comes down.

11

A crane is a large machine
that helps build tall buildings.
A crane has a long arm.
A pulley is attached to the arm.
The crane driver uses the machine
to pull down on a rope or chain
and lift up heavy things
that are needed to build the new building.

This crane is being used to help build a tall skyscraper.

13

A flagpole has a pulley at the top. The flag is attached to the rope. When you pull the rope, you can move the flag up and down the flagpole.

15

PULLEYS: PAST AND PRESENT

In the past, people did not have big machines with motors. They used pulleys to build and move many things.

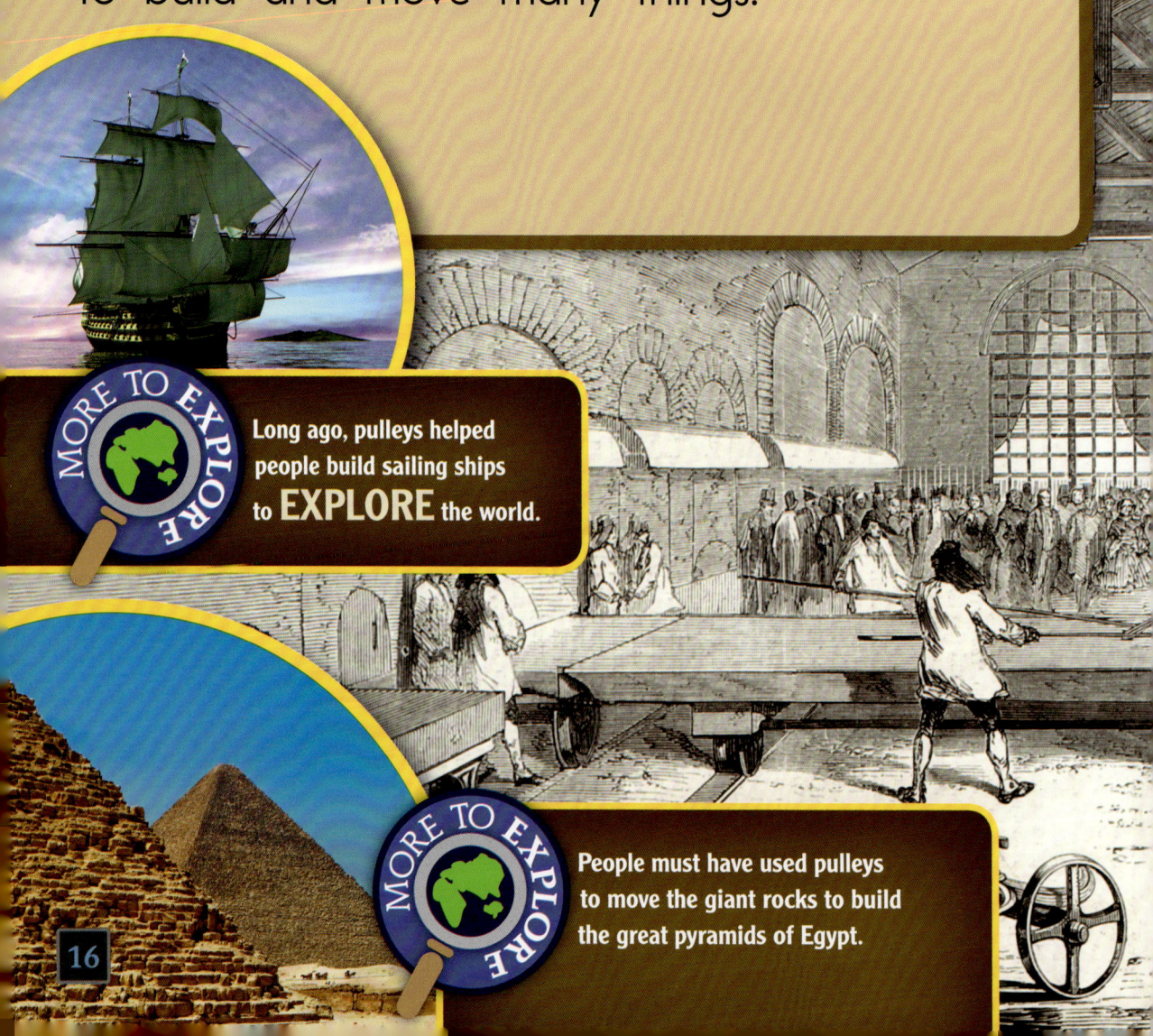

MORE TO EXPLORE
Long ago, pulleys helped people build sailing ships to **EXPLORE** the world.

MORE TO EXPLORE
People must have used pulleys to move the giant rocks to build the great pyramids of Egypt.

17

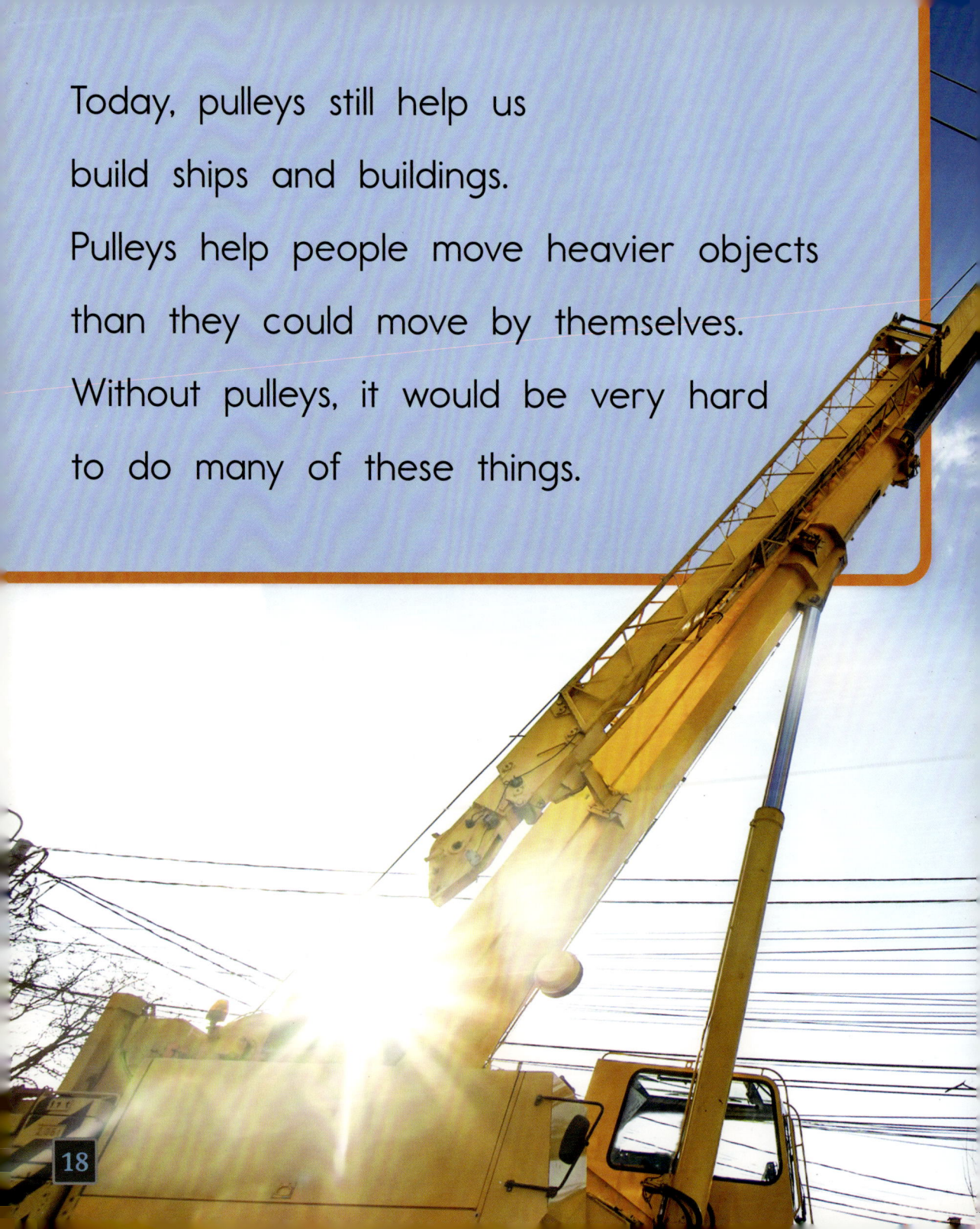

Today, pulleys still help us build ships and buildings.

Pulleys help people move heavier objects than they could move by themselves.

Without pulleys, it would be very hard to do many of these things.

19

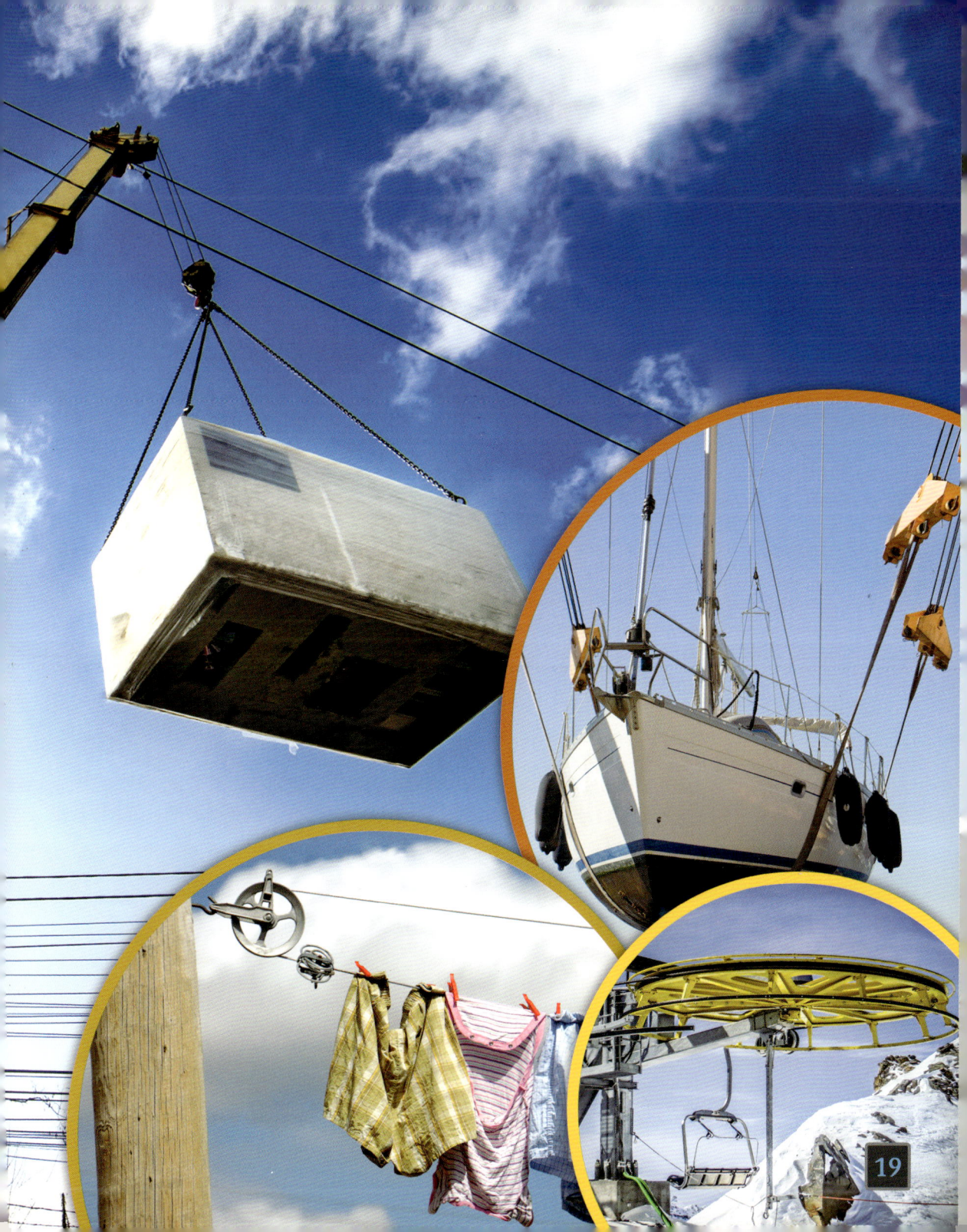

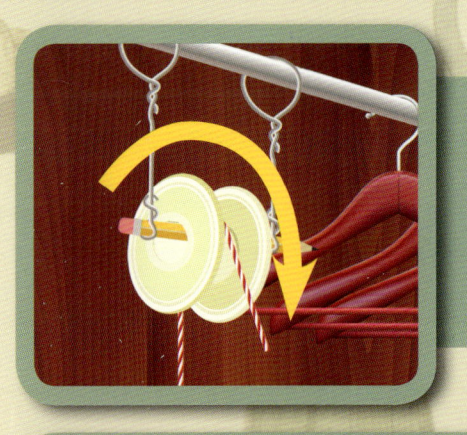

Step Three
Loop free end of string over wheel.

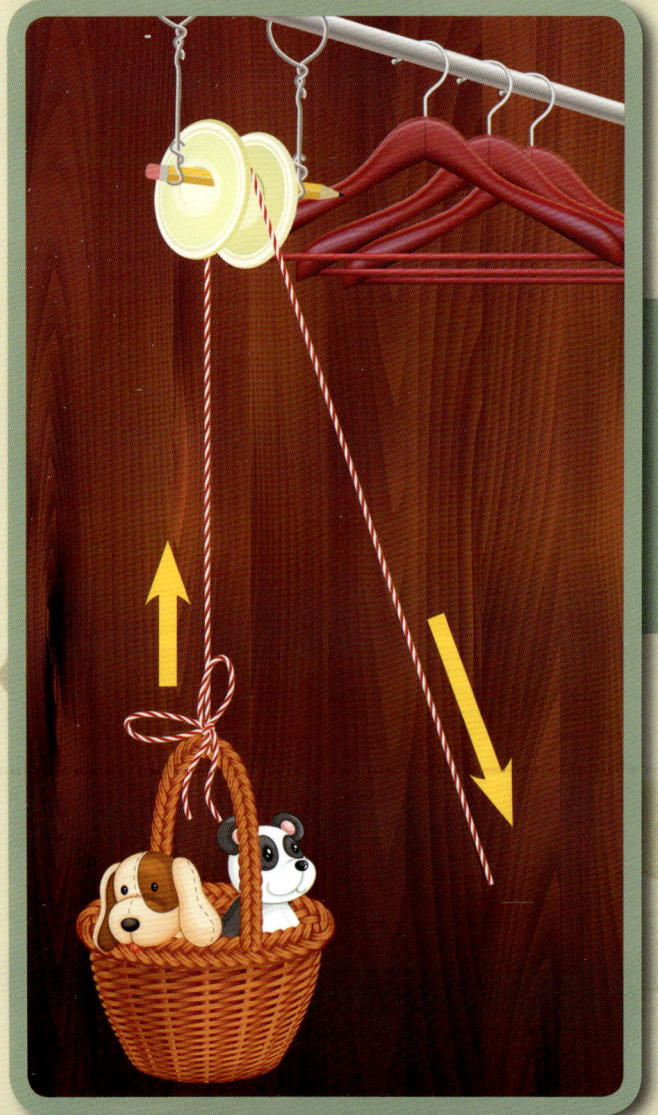

Step Four
Pull the free end of the string to lift the basket!

How to Make Your Own Pulley

Items needed:
- ribbon spool
- pencil
- wire
- string
- basket

Step One
Put the pencil through the ribbon spool and attach it with wire to a high place.

Step Two
Attach string to basket handle.

GLOSSARY

attached
joined to another thing

blinds
window coverings that keep out light

explore
to travel to a place to learn about it

groove
a long narrow cut in a surface

load
something that is carried

release
to let go

INDEX

attached 2, 14
arm 12–13
blinds 8
build 12, 16
cranes 12–13
explore 16
flagpole 14
groove 2–3
heavy 2, 4, 6, 12
lift 6, 8, 10, 12
load 4
parts (of a pulley) 3
pyramids 16
release 8, 10
sailboat 10–11
well 6–7
wheel 2–3, 8, 10